A New Job For Stan

Written by Jenny Feely

Illustrated by Stephen Axelsen

Flying Start
to Literacy®

Contents

Chapter 1:

A job for everyone   4

Chapter 2:

A sad farewell   10

Chapter 3:

A daring plan   14

Chapter 4:

Into the air   20

Chapter 1:
A job for everyone

Everyone at the circus had a job.

Bobo was the clown.
Harry was the strong man.
And Lizzie flew high in the air
on the trapeze.

And Stan's job was to take the circus posters from town to town on his motorcycle.

Stan loved riding his motorcycle and he loved his job. But Stan wanted a job in the big top – just like his friends.

Every day, Stan did stunts
on his motorcycle. He rode
up ramps and did handstands
and flips on his motorcycle.

And every day he got
a little better.

But when Stan showed his motorcycle stunts to the ringmaster, she shook her head.

"No, Stan. You have a job," she said. "Your job is to take the circus posters to each town. It is an important job and you are very good at it."

But Stan was not happy.
Every day, he watched his friends
in the big top and every day,
he became sadder and sadder.

Chapter 2:
A sad farewell

So Stan packed his bags and rode away from the circus.

"I will find a new circus," he said. "I will find a circus where I can do stunts on my motorcycle."

Stan was sad to leave his friends. He looked back just one last time – and that is when Stan saw the smoke coming out of the big top.

"Oh no," he said. "My friends are in danger. I must help them."

Stan quickly raced back to the circus.

Chapter 3:
A daring plan

When Stan got to the big top, everyone was throwing buckets of water on the flames.

"Lizzie is up on the trapeze," yelled the ringmaster. "We can't get her down."

The flames were getting bigger and bigger. If they didn't get Lizzie down soon, it would be too late.

Then Stan had an idea.

"I can get Lizzie down," said
Stan. "But I will need help."

Stan told everyone what to do.
They quickly made a ramp.

The ringmaster pulled back one side of the tent. Bobo ran around and pulled back the other side of the tent.

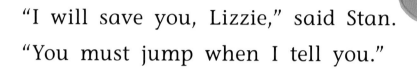

"I will save you, Lizzie," said Stan.
"You must jump when I tell you."

"I can't!" said Lizzie.
"I'm too frightened. I might fall."

"Trust me," said Stan. "I won't
let you fall."

"Hurry!" yelled
the ringmaster.

Chapter 4: Into the air

Stan got on his motorcycle and took off towards the ramp as fast as he could. His motorcycle went faster and faster. He went up the ramp and into the air.

Stan flew over the flames.

"Get ready to jump," he yelled to Lizzie, as he flew towards her.

Stan stood up and reached out his hands. Lizzie reached out her hands. Stan grabbed on tight.

"I've got you," he said. He flipped Lizzie onto the back of the motorcycle.

Down the motorcycle went and landed on the ramp on the other side of the big top. They rode out of the burning tent.

Lizzie was saved!

And so Stan stayed with the circus.

Every day, he still takes the circus posters from town to town on his motorcycle.

But every night, he flies high above the ground, through the ring of fire to save Lizzie!